# Why Question Jesus

ADEDAYO ADENIJI

Scripture quotations marked NIV are taken from the Holy Bible, New International
Version®. NIV®. Copyright © 1973, 1978, 1984 by International Bible Society.
Used by permission of Zondervan. All rights reserved. [Biblica]

AuthorHouse™ UK
1663 Liberty Drive
Bloomington, IN 47403  USA
www.authorhouse.co.uk
UK TFN: 0800 0148641 (Toll Free inside the UK)
UK Local: 02036 956322 (+44 20 3695 6322 from outside the UK)

Because of the dynamic nature of the Internet, any web addresses or links contained in
this book may have changed since publication and may no longer be valid. The views
expressed in this work are solely those of the author and do not necessarily reflect the
views of the publisher, and the publisher hereby disclaims any responsibility for them.

Any people depicted in stock imagery provided by Getty Images are models,
and such images are being used for illustrative purposes only.
Certain stock imagery © Getty Images.

This book is printed on acid-free paper.

ISBN: 978-1-6655-8723-5 (sc)
ISBN: 978-1-6655-8722-8 (e)

Print information available on the last page.

Published by AuthorHouse  03/11/2021

**author**HOUSE®

# About the Author:

I am still asking questions about my purpose in life, yes this God given life, with it's ups and downs, past, present and future dimensions and the search for truth.

My friends call me Dayo.

Adedayo is a Nigerian name.

I was born in Highgate, London and brought up in Peckham, London.

Having a brother as a twin developed my character in an interesting way.

My parents have passed away, leaving four children and six grandchildren.

After school, I gained a Higher National Diploma in Applied Biology.

Since then my CV is filled with a variety of jobs from being a laboratory technician to currently working as a sales assistant.

God has changed my life since my baptism in 1987, for the better.

I'm still asking questions, and on this human journey am understanding a little, about the meaning of life, and as Jesus says in

Luke 10:10
"The thief comes only to steal and kill and destroy; I
have come that they may live life to the full"

As God helped and is still helping me grow as a Christian, the gifts that He blessed me with grew too, especially poetry and song writing.

Even up to this day, I am still asking questions about life, truth and God the Creator.

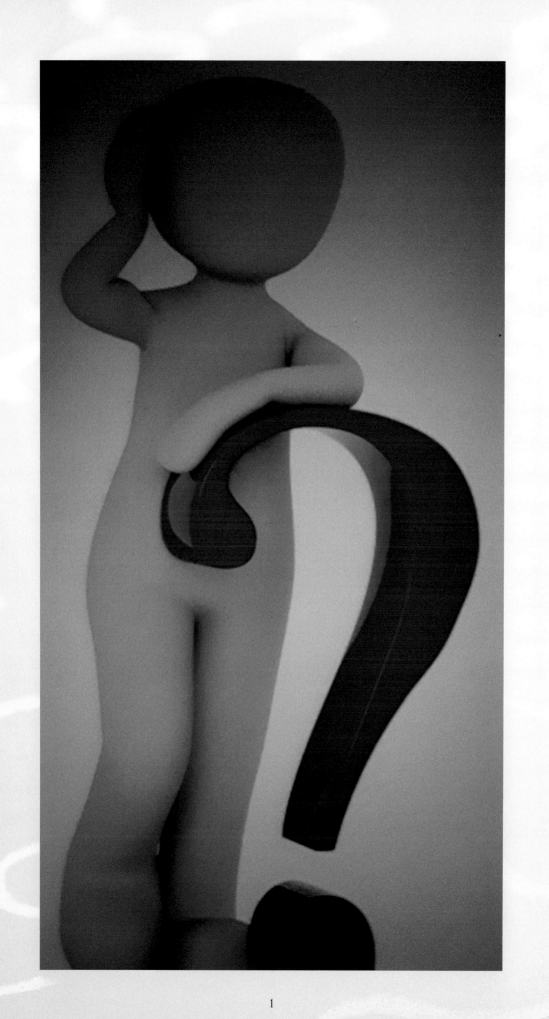

THE ALPHA OMEGA, WHAT A MYSTERY
THE FATHER SON AND SPIRIT, TRINITY
FREE WILL AND THE SOUL'S ETERNITY
AND CHOOSING ONE'S OWN DESTINY

## Analogy:

Water for example exists as ice, liquid and steam.

# CONVERSATION

Who are they?

Colossians 4:6

Let your conversation be always full of grace, seasoned with salt,
so that you may know how to answer everyone.

There are so many repeated questions about why God does what He does, why Jesus does what He does, why the Holy Spirit does what He does and why the disciples of Jesus do what they did do.

## WHY QUESTION JESUS?

If you are the Son of God, can you change stones to bread
To bow down and worship you, with no where to lay your head
Are you really the one claimed to be born King of the Jews
Head over every authority, power, dominion and rule.

Could this actually be the Son of David
Isn't then the kingdom shrinking and divided
Because of Herodias, John was arrested
So couldn't this really be the man called John the
Baptist

So from this prophet without any honour
What wisdom, love and miraculous power
Isn't this then the carpenter's son
With brothers, Judas, James, Joseph and Simon And His sisters, who really are they
His mother's name, isn't it Mary
How do you know me, people asked Him
Jesus replied, "you shall see even greater things"

Even Nicodemus asked at night, but not during the day
Are you really going to raise the temple in just three days
"Prove your authority with the miracles that you do"
Argued in disbelief, many of the unbelieving
Jews

And with the invalid, who for 38 years remained so ill
The Jews again asked Jesus, "why on the Sabbath heal"
The Samaritan woman thought, that Jacob was greater
The disciples asked Jesus, "why are you even talking with her"

The following quote is taken from 'Tricky Trinity Questions' by the Author, Colin Adams

"The way in which God is one is different from the way in which He is three...God is not one something and also somehow three of the same somethings. If we were to say, 'God is one person and God is three persons', this would be a contradiction. But the way in which He is one is not the same as the way in which he is three. He is one in name and nature and he is three in person. This may be - OK, is – hard for us to understand, but at the very least we need to recognise that it is not contradictory."

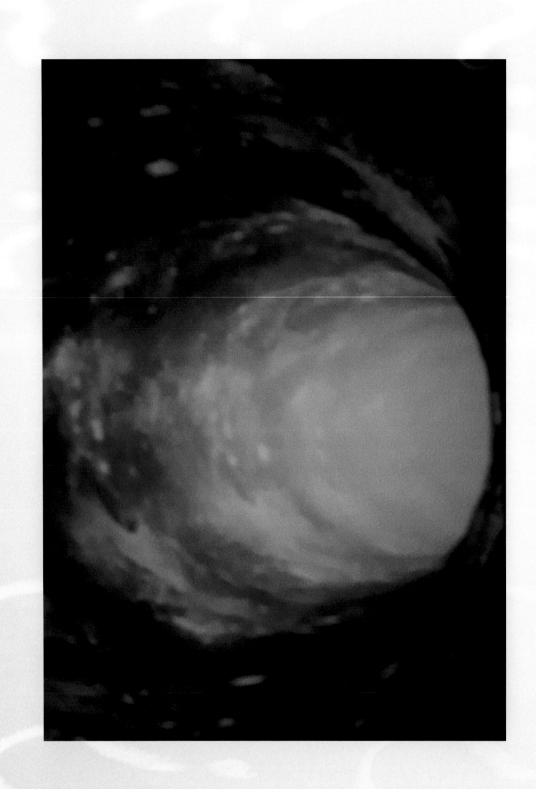

SPACE AND TIME CREATED
PAST, PRESENT AND FUTURE
JESUS RESURRECTED
BY GOD, LOVING FATHER

## Analogy:

Imagine two doors. One labelled "Hell" and the other "Heaven". You decide to open the door to Hell just to see what it's like. Upon opening that door, you see a single room with one table and people surrounding it. As you look closer, you also notice that the people do not possess any arms. However they have food in front of them. But without any arms, they are starving and cannot eat properly.

You then open the door to Heaven. Like Hell, there is also a table and people surrounding it. And to your surprise they are missing arms as well. But what you really notice is that instead of eternally starving, each person is using their mouth to grasp a spoon and is helping to feed the person beside them. Everyone patiently takes turns and nobody is starving.

# OTHER SIDE

How can He come from Heaven?

Hebrews 9:28 so Christ was sacrificed once to take away the sins of many people; and He will appear a second time, not to bear sin, but to bring salvation to those who are waiting for Him.

There are so many repeated questions about why God does what He does, Why Jesus does what He does, Why the Holy Spirit does what He does and why the disciples of Jesus do what they did do.

WHY QUESTION JESUS?

The Jews still asked Jesus, "how can He come from Heaven"
Why should they remember all of the prophets and listen

The disciples asked about food for the people to eat
They just wanted the crowd to go away and retreat

The Jews, well they just continued to grumble and argue
Crowds asked Jesus about works and signs of miracles

Even the disciples asked, "who can accept this hard teaching"
Because they were offended that Jesus would be ascending

"Where is that man", the Jews asked at the feast
Jesus went to the temple courts and began to teach

Simon Peter said, "Lord to whom shall we go
We see and believe the Holy One of God you know"

Such learning without having studied, the Jews amazed
And wanted to kill Him, yet He escaped their seize

The temple guards couldn't even bring Jesus in
"Where will He go, that we cannot find Him"

Pharisees and teachers of the law came from Jerusalem
"Why do your disciples not wash, breaking the elders tradition"

The disciples asked, "why are the Pharisees so offended"
"They are blind guides my heavenly Father has not planted"

The Canaanite expected Jesus to have mercy
So Jesus called her a dog, though she suffered terribly

Of the sheep of Israel, this woman was definitely not
Yet Jesus saw her great faith, and still called her a dog.

Taken from the book by Alan W Gomes
www.kregel.com popular author Tim Keller put it like this:-

"The way you live now is completely controlled by what you believe about the future"

What you truly believe about the life beyond - or do not believe about it – determines your loves, your motivations, your goals and how you direct your energies in this one. It cannot help but do so.

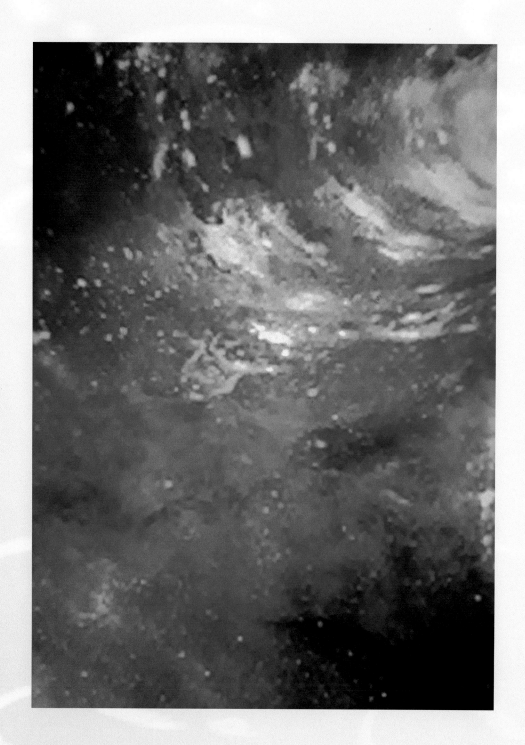

LIFE AND IT'S DIFFERENT DIMENSIONS
WHAT IS TRUTH? ANOTHER QUESTION
SIN'S GUILT IN EVERY GENERATION
UNDERSTAND THE HUMAN CONDITION

## Analogy:

The ant on the telephone pole is often used to entice people into the extra-dimensional view point of string theory.

The ants on the telephone cables shows that if something is small enough then it can easily go unnoticed.

# ARRIVAL

Where are you going?

John 13:36

Simon Peter asked him, "Lord, where are you going?"

Jesus replied, "Where I am going, you cannot follow now, but you will follow later."

There are so many repeated questions about why God does what He does, why Jesus does what He does, why the Holy Spirit does what He does and why the disciples of Jesus do what they did do.

## WHY QUESTION JESUS?

With the feeding of the four thousand that Jesus fed
The disciples didn't know where to get enough bread
Asked about Elijah first, and then John the Baptist
The Pharisees and Sadduces were looking for
Jesus to test

Even with the miracles, what were they really accomplishing
When some Jews saw a dead man that Jesus was raising
"What do you think, isn't He coming to the feast at all"
It was the Jewish Passover and the cleansing ceremonial

The disciples said, "you are going back, where the Jews tried to stone you"
And Thomas said, "to die with Him, let's also go"
Judas who would betray His friend Jesus, with a single kiss
Asked "why not sell the perfume as it's too
expensive"

Mary loved Jesus, using the perfume to wipe His feet
Asking more questions before the Passover feast
The crowds with palm branches for Jesus arriving at the feast
Peter asked, "Lord are you going to wash my whole body and feet"

Thomas again asked Jesus, "Lord where are you going"
Peter said, "Lord my life, you i am following"
Phillip asked Jesus, "Lord show us all of the Father"
And Judas said, "why show yourself to the world no longer"

"Have the authorities concluded, that Jesus is the Christ"
And that on the third day, He is going to rise
"When the Christ comes, no one will know where He is from"
No one would lay a hand on Him, His time had not yet come

# Quote:- science.howstuffworks.com

Question, how can our brains see the fourth dimension (Paragraph 5)

If we can't see the fourth dimension to time travel, and if we can't see the fourth dimension, then what's the point of knowing about it?

Understanding these higher dimensions is of importance to the mathematicians and physicists because it helps them understand the world. String theory, for example relies on at least 10 dimensions to remain viable.[source: Groleau]. For these researchers, the answers to complies problems in the 3-D world may be found in the next dimension-and beyond.

Because we only know life in 3-D, our brains don't understand how to look for anything more.

WHY QUESTION JESUS, WHY QUESTION HIM
LORD, LIAR OR LUNATIC OR ETERNAL KING
WHY SHOULD WE WORSHIP HIM DEEP WITHIN
WHO SAVED ALL HUMANS FROM THE HORRORS OF SIN

## Analogy:

A blog by Justin Taylor www.thegospelcoalition.org

C.S Lewis popularized the argument that Jesus was either a liar or a lunatic or the Lord.

In the mid-nineteenth century the Scottish

Christian preacher "Rabbi" John Duncan(17961870) formulated what he called a "trilemma". In Colloquial Peripatetica(p.109) we see Duncan's argument from 1859-1860.

Christ either deceived mankind by conscious fraud or he was himself deluded and selfdeceived, or he was Divine. There is no getting out of this trilemma. It is inexorable.

There is no need for us to prove if Jesus of Nazareth is God or not. All we have to do is find out if He is lunatic or liar. If He is neither. He must be the Son of God.

# REPEAT

Seeing you no more then seeing you.

John 16:16

"In a little while you will see me no more, and then after a little while you will see me"

There are so many repeated questions about why God does what He does, why Jesus does what He does, why the Holy Spirit does what He does, and why the disciples of Jesus do what they did do.

# WHY QUESTION JESUS?

There are so many repeated questions about why God does what He does, why Jesus does what He does, why the Holy Spirit does what He does and why the disciples of Jesus do what they did do.

The Pharisees asked Jesus, "where is your Father"
Jesus only wanted them to be set free, for ever and ever
The woman caught in adultery, Jesus had this to say
"No one has condemned you woman, where are they?"
The Jews asked Jesus, "who do you think you are?
You must be demon possessed, not a prophet, but a sinner"
The Pharisees said to Jesus, "are we blind too?"
So Jesus healed the blind man, who then became a disciple

The Jews divided said, "look why listen to him If you are the Christ the Messiah, then make it plain"
The unbelief of the Jews, with their heads in suspense
Didn't believe Jesus, whom God the Father sent

The meaning of seeing you no more, then seeing you
Disciples said to Jesus, having no idea or any clue
Even the meaning of their, grief turning to joy
So that the Son and Father may be enjoyed and glorified

"Is this the way you answer the high priest Caiaphas"
Jesus accused of many charges, and struck right in the face
Pilate asked, "are you really then King of the Jews
What have you done, I have the power to release you"

Pilate asked Jesus about truth and where He came from
Yet handed Him over to die by crucifixion
After all these questions, Jesus says, "Follow me" And for those who doubt, "Well stop doubting and believe"

# Quote:

A man who was merely a man and said the sort of things Jesus said would not be a great moral teacher. He would either be a lunatic - on the level with the man who says he is a poached egg or else he would be the Devil of Hell. You must make your choice.

Either this man was, and is, the Son of God; or else a mad man or something worse. You can shut Him up for a fool, you can spit at Him and kill Him as a demon; or you can fall at His feet and call Him Lord and God.

But let us not come with any patronising nonsense about His being a great human teacher. He has not left that open to us.

He did not intend to.

C.S Lewis

Hope that you have enjoyed these poems about why question Jesus and that you can start questioning not only Jesus, but your own heart too.

Printed in the United States
by Baker & Taylor Publisher Services